Even though we may not look the same on the outside, we are all the same on the inside!

Beautiful Me Inside and Out

First American Edition 2019

Published in the United States by Bello Moi Publishing,
2901 Clint Moore Rd, #324 Boca Raton. Fl. 33496

Copyright © 2019 Bello Moi Publishing
All rights reserved.

Without limiting the rights under copyright reserved above, no part of this publication may be reproduced, stored in a retrieval system, or transmitted in any form or by any means. No part of this book may be reproduced in any written, electronic, recording, or photocopying form without prior permission of both the author and publisher of this book, except by a reviewer who may quote brief passages in a review.

ISBN-13: 978-0692145616

Bello Moi books are available at a special discount when purchased in bulk for sales promotions, premiums, fundraising or educational use.
For details, contact:
Bello Moi Publishing
2901 Clint Moore Rd, #324 Boca Raton. Fl. 33496
or by email at info@bellomoi.com or 561.654.8463

Discover more at www.bellomoi.com

"Mommy, Why Are They Wearing That?" presents the positive message that teaches children (and adults) the reasons and traditions behind various religious outfits. Children are undoubtedly going to stare and question fascinating religious garments. The book ultimately encourages people to not pass judgment and to respect others.

Jasper was at the park with his mom. He was swinging on the swing set when his mom caught him staring at a family wearing unusual clothes. "Jasper! Stop staring. That is not nice," his mom said. "Sorry, Mommy, but why are they wearing that?" Jasper asked. Jasper was curious.

Jasper's mom explained it is part of their religion. They are Orthodox Jews. Jewish clothing customs are a large part of Judaism and Jewish life. The men wear a skullcap called a kippah or yarmulke on their heads. Some men wear large black hats of different styles and shapes. The women wear skirts that cover the knees and shirts that cover the collarbone and elbows. Jewish women who are married will often cover their heads with a hat, scarf or wig. They believe in being plain on the outside and beautiful on the inside.

Jasper and his mom decided to get a slice of pizza. Jasper wanted pizza with pepperoni. As Jasper was getting ready to take his first bite of pizza, he saw a man wearing a cloth on the top of his head. "Mommy, why is he wearing that?" Jasper asked his mom.

Jasper's mom explained it is part of their religion. He is Sikh. The cloth on his head is called a dastar. In the Sikh religion, men commonly wear a peaked turban that covers their long hair, which is never cut. Sikh men do not cut their beards. Sikh women wear head scarves to cover their long hair. When entering their place of worship, they cover their long hair and remove their shoes in respect to their religion.

On their way home, Jasper and his mom visited a toy store. He was so excited to pick out a new toy. He didn't know if he should choose a dinosaur or robot. As he was reaching for a Tyrannosaurus rex, a woman with her head covered was standing next to him. Jasper grabbed the Tyrannosaurus rex and said to his mom, "Mommy, why is she wearing that?"

Jasper's mom explained it is part of their religion. She is Muslim. The women in the Islamic religion cover their hair with a head covering called a hijab. Some wear a burka, which covers their face. Many of the women cover their entire bodies with a long robe dress when they are outside of their home. Muslim men also cover their entire bodies with cloth robes that do not fall below their ankles, so the cloth does not touch the dirty ground. The purpose of the covering is to create modesty, dignity and respect.

The next day, Jasper and his mom took their dog Max for a walk. Jasper wanted to hold Max's leash. Max stopped to sniff a fire hydrant and Jasper's mom caught Jasper staring at a man and a woman. "Mommy, why are they wearing that?" Jasper asked his mom.

Jasper's mom explained it is part of their religion. They are Christians. Jasper's mom explained that they were walking near a church. The man is called a priest or father. He wears a long robe with a cross. The woman is called a nun or sister. She wears a full-length black and white dress with a veil or headdress called a habit. The priest and nun dress this way to show their dedication to their religion.

Jasper was invited to his friend Olivia's birthday party. Jasper helped wrap her present in bright pink wrapping paper. He was very excited to give Olivia her present. Jasper and his mom arrived at the house and rang the doorbell. The lady who answered the door had a red circle on her forehead and was dressed in an outfit that Jasper had never seen before. Jasper turned around to his mom and asked, "Mommy, why is she wearing that?"

Jasper's mom explained it is part of their religion. She is a Hindu. Olivia's parents are from India. The dot on her forehead is called a bindi. The bindi is worn by married women as a commitment to long-life and the well-being of their husbands. The dress Olivia's mom is wearing is known as a sari. The sari is a long piece of fabric that is draped and tucked into the waistband. Women who prefer to cover their heads might wear a long scarf called a chunni. Hindu men often wear a long cotton shirt called a kurta covered by a dhoti, which is also a long piece of material that ties around the waist to cover most of their legs. The Hindus believe in truth and that what you do in this life will affect what will happen in your after life.

Jasper and his mom walked to a pond to feed the fish. As Jasper threw the fish food to the jumping fish, he saw a group of people exercising. To Jasper, it looked like they were doing a slow dance. The people exercising wore dark blue pants and shirts. Jasper turned to his mom and asked, "Mommy, why are they wearing that?"

Jasper's mom explained it is part of their religion. They are Taoists. They are practicing martial arts. There is no special clothing that must always be worn, but the color red is very important. It is a lucky color. A Taoist robe might be worn for a festival. It would be made of silk with bright colors. In their religion, staying healthy and living a long life is important. Also, the practice of Ying and Yang, opposites like hot and cold, are often taught.

Jasper and his mom drove to the airport to pick up Jasper's dad. Jasper could hardly wait to see his dad. His dad has been out of town for two weeks on a business trip. As they waited at the airport, Jasper saw two bald men wearing orange robes. Jasper was about to point at the men, but stopped, as he knew pointing at people wasn't nice. Instead he turned to his mom and asked, "Mommy, why are they wearing that?

Jasper's mom explained it is part of their religion. They are Buddhists. The robes worn by the Buddhist monks may be in different colors but they are always very simple. The purpose of the simple robes is to represent the monks' simple lifestyle. The monks believe shaving their own heads shows a commitment to a holy life. Buddhists also wear a mala, a bracelet that has 108 beads. The beaded bracelet is used in the Buddhist religion to help focus the mind. Buddhists believe every action causes an effect, so they always try to do the right thing.

Jasper's mom explained it is part of their religion. He is a Jain. Jasper's mom explained in the Jainism religion, the monks and nuns wear plain white robes. They wear white masks to cover their mouths. They believe the mask protects them from swallowing any living creature, like flies, by accident. Some Jains carry a broom to sweep bugs out of the way, so they will not hurt them. The men shave their heads and the women cover their hair. The reason Jains do not wear shoes is to avoid crushing bugs or insects on the ground. In the Jainism religion they believe in nonviolence and a respect for all life.

Jasper's mom tucked Jasper into bed. She could tell something was still on his mind. Jasper was still thinking about all the different religious clothing he had seen.

Jasper's mom told him, "There are many different religions. Religion is like a fingerprint. Everyone is slightly different. All religions involve different dress, rituals, traditions, practices and beliefs that are special to a particular faith."

Despite the differences in how we look or dress, or what we eat or celebrate, we are the same. We are all people.

Goodnight.

DEDICATION

I wrote this book for my grandsons, Camden and Sage. They love to have me read bedtime stories. Our reading time is not only for enjoyment but also for learning something new. I dedicate this book to Charlie Bella. She always makes me smile and has a special place in my heart.

Carol Lezell

 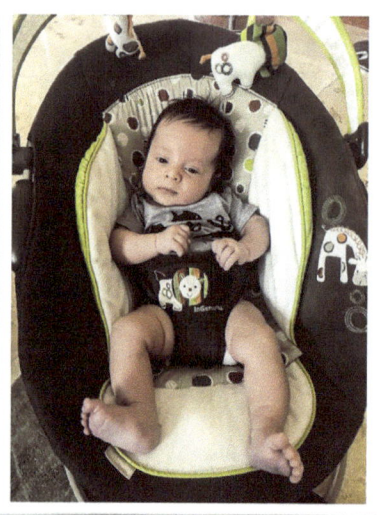 

I dedicate this book to my son, Sage. I want to impress upon him, at a young age, never to point at someone who was wearing something unfamiliar. I was also interested and fascinated by the different clothing of other cultures and religions. I wanted to share this with him. Also, I dedicate this to my husband, Kevin, for his continuous encouragement and inspiration.

Logan Lezell

ABOUT THE AUTHORS

Carol Lezell is the mother of three children. She always loved reading to her children. She never knew who enjoyed it more, she or the kids. Carol is also co-author with Logan of a Healthy Recipes for Healthy Skin Cookbook and co-owner of a natural skincare company, Bello Moi.

Logan Lezell loves traveling and learning about different cultures, customs and religions. After a trip to Morocco and Kuala Lumpur, she was inspired to write a book about the religious significance of clothing. Logan is also co-author of Healthy Recipes for Healthy Skin Cookbook and owner of Bello Moi, a natural skincare company.

www.ingramcontent.com/pod-product-compliance
Lightning Source LLC
Chambersburg PA
CBHW061401090426
42743CB00002B/108